Social Skills
Communication

Mini-Books to Teach Essential Social Skills

Carson Dellosa Education
Greensboro, North Carolina

Credits

Author: Christine Schwab
Illustrations: Pam Thayer, Julie Kinlaw, Erik Huffine, J.J. Rudisill

Key Education®
An imprint of Carson Dellosa Education
PO Box 35665
Greensboro, NC 27425 USA
carsondellosa.com

ISBN 978-1-4838-5692-6
01-335197784

Table of Contents

Introduction

Social skills are important. They are like good manners. Using them properly makes it easier to relate to other people with positive outcomes. Children with age-appropriate social skills can more effectively communicate, make decisions, solve problems, create and maintain successful relationships, and manage their own behavior. A lack of age-appropriate social skills interferes with children's relationships with other children, their teachers, and their family members.

Social skills do not come naturally to all children. But, social skills can be shaped. Social narratives—short stories that focus on specific social skills or desired behaviors—are useful tools to this end. They can be written or modified to meet any specific challenge.

Ideas for Using the Materials in This Book

Making the Mini-Books

This book focuses on tasks that are important in building essential skills. These pages present 13 mini-books that highlight and reinforce common behavior expectations. The illustrations are simple and printed in black and white so that children can color them. This interactive component helps children make the mini-books "their own" books.

The story pages are perforated and can be reproduced (two-sided) or assembled as single copies. Some children can cut apart and assemble the pages themselves, then staple the pages together on the left side of the books. (Check that the pages are in the correct order and help children if needed.) You may also choose to bind the books by using a hole punch and yarn or small metal rings.

Once the books are assembled, have children read their completed social narratives aloud. If a child cannot read independently, read the lines to the child. Following the first reading, have children "sign" their title pages and color the illustrations with crayons or markers. Reread the stories as needed. Over time, the narratives will become more familiar.

Repetition

New behaviors become more deeply ingrained each time they are practiced, so it is important to encourage children to read and reread their social narratives (aloud to another person). A goal chart is printed on the back page of each story to help children keep track of their progress toward a goal of reading the social story 10 times. This book concludes with award certificates for achievement and effort.

In This Book

Each mini-book in this book focuses on an important developmental social skill. They can be used in any order and as frequently as needed.

These social narratives are written in simple language so that they can be easily understood and assimilated. We hope they will prove to be an invaluable tool in shaping children's behavior.

Saying "Hello" and "Goodbye"

by _____

I can say "hello" to my family when I get up in the morning.

2 It is good manners to say "hello" when I see someone I know.
I can also say "hi."

I can say "hello" to my teachers and friends at school.
4 I can say "hello" to all of the people I see in my day.

Sometimes, I see someone I do not know.
Then, it is good manners to say, "Hello. My name
is _____."

5

Saying "hello" and "goodbye" helps me to be friendly.
It helps me show my good manners.
I feel proud when I am friendly and show good manners.

7

6

It is also good manners to say "goodbye."
I can say "goodbye" to my family when I leave for school.
I can say "goodbye" at school when I go home.

I will work on meeting
my goal - 10 ✔'s!

Make a ✔ each time you read your story.

8

Asking Questions

by _____

I can ask a friend, "What did you do last night?"
My friend will enjoy telling me a story about his evening.

(3)

It is good to ask questions.
Questions are sentences that ask about something.
I will learn something after I ask a question.

2

I can ask my family, "Where are we going?"
When they answer, I can plan my trip.
I can ask my family about a lot of things.

4

I can ask my teacher, "Will you please help me?"
Then, my teacher will know that I need help.
I can ask my teacher about a lot of things.

5

Questions help me find out things.
Questions help me get along with others.
It is important to ask questions.

7

(6) I can ask a friend, "Will you play ball with me?"
Then, my friend and I can have fun together.

I will work on meeting
my goal - 10 ✔'s!

Make a ✔ each time you read your story.

Asking Permission

by _____

It is important to ask permission for many things at school.
It is most important to ask for permission before leaving the room.
I can never leave the room without asking for permission.

(3)

Asking permission is when you ask if it is OK to do something.
Sometimes I ask, "May I have a drink, please?"
Or, "May I please go to the restroom?"

2

If I want to borrow something that belongs to my teacher, I will ask,
"May I please borrow that?"

4

It is never OK to take something that belongs to someone else without asking permission.
I will ask permission before I touch anything.

⑤

My teachers and friends feel happy when I ask permission.
I am proud of myself when I remember the rules.

⑦

(6) When my teachers or friends say "yes" or "OK," I know I can borrow or touch or take something.
If they say "no," I will forget about it and walk away.

I will work on meeting
my goal - 10 ✔'s!

Make a ✔ each time you read your story.

Taking Turns in Conversation

by _____

In a conversation, it is important for each person to talk about the same thing.
I must pay attention to what the other person says.

③

(2) When two people talk to each other, one person talks first.
Then, the other person talks.
This is called having a conversation.

(4) People take turns talking in a conversation.
They don't interrupt or talk when the other person is talking.

I can have a conversation about many things.
I can talk about things I like.
Something I like to talk about is _____.

(5)

Friends talk about many things.
I will remember to take turns talking and listening.
This is how friends talk.

(7)

6

I will talk about something I like.
Then, I will listen to my friend talk about it too.
Next, it is my turn to talk again.

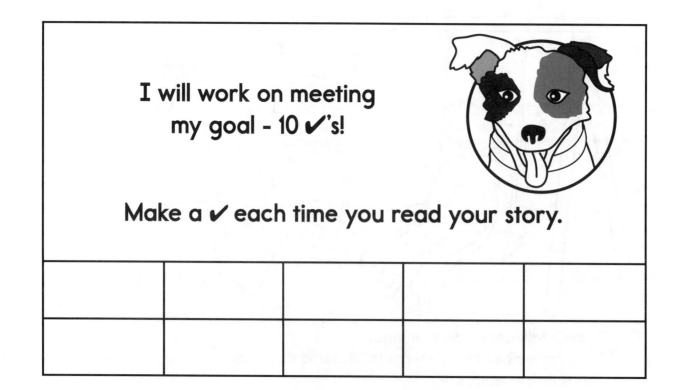

I will work on meeting
my goal - 10 ✔'s!

Make a ✔ each time you read your story.

Sticking to the Topic

by _____

We will talk about one topic.
The topic is the main thing we will talk about.

(3)

(2) When I want to talk to my friends,
I can start by telling them about something I like.
Or, I can ask them a question.

(4) A topic might be a sport, a food, a vacation, or a superhero.
This one thing is called the topic.

I can ask questions about the topic.
Or, I can tell what I know about the topic.

5

My friends will like to talk to me if I stick to the topic.
That is how good conversation happens.
This is what friends do.

7

6 This is not the time for me to talk about something else.
This is the time to stick to the topic.

I will work on meeting
my goal - 10 ✔'s!

Make a ✔ each time you read your story.

Making Eye Contact

by _____

This is called making eye contact.
When I make eye contact, people know I am listening.

③

(2) It is important to look at people when they talk to me.
If I do not, they will think I am not listening to them.
They will think I am rude.

I feel shy.

Sometimes, it is hard for me to make eye contact.
I might feel shy.
I want to look away or look at something else.

(4)

26

Sometimes, I would rather look at the floor than at people's eyes.
Sometimes, I would rather look anywhere else!

(5)

Everyone is happy when I make eye contact.
They know I am paying attention.
They will want to talk to me again.

(7)

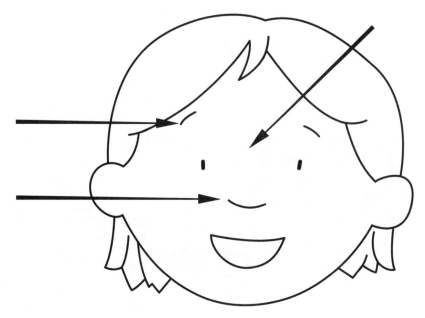

6 If I cannot look at people's eyes, I can look at their faces. I can look at their noses, their eyebrows, or the spaces between their eyes.

- -

I will work on meeting my goal - 10 ✔'s!

Make a ✔ each time you read your story.

Telling the Truth

by _____

Telling the truth means that I will say exactly what I see.
I will say exactly what I feel or think.
I will tell the truth.

(3)

(2) It is important for people to tell the truth.
I will always try to tell the truth.

When I do not tell the truth, I make people feel sad.
I hurt people's feelings when I do not tell the truth.

Sometimes, I feel afraid to tell the truth.
I worry that I will get in trouble if I tell the truth.

(5)

When I tell the truth, my family and teachers are proud of me.
I can be proud too when I tell the truth.

(7)

It's always best to tell the truth.

6 I will do my best to tell the truth, even if I feel afraid.
It is always best to tell the truth.

- -

I will work on meeting
my goal - 10 ✔'s!

Make a ✔ each time you read your story.

Using Good Words

by _____

It is important to use good words when I talk to my friends, teachers, and family.
It is important to use good words everywhere.

2 Some words are good.
Some words are bad.
I have good manners when I say only good words.

4 When something goes wrong, I might want to say a bad word.
Instead, I can say, "Oh, man!" or "Too bad!" or "Shoot!"

Sometimes, when I feel angry or hurt, I feel like saying bad words. Some of these words are swear words.

(5)

Please.

Thank you.

I'm sorry.

Excuse me.

Saying bad words can get me in trouble.
I will do my best to use good words no matter how I feel.
Everyone is proud of me when I use good words.

(7)

6 Swear words are not OK at school, at home, or in a restaurant.
Swear words are not OK anywhere!

- -

I will work on meeting
my goal - 10 ✔'s!

Make a ✔ each time you read your story.

Things to Talk About

by _____

I don't always know what to say to other kids.
But, I can practice things to say.

(3)

Sometimes, I like to sit quietly by myself.
Sometimes, I like to talk to other kids.
I like to have friends.

(2)

If it is lunchtime, I can say something like, "Your lunch looks good!"

(4)

If we are waiting in line, I can ask, "What are you going
to eat for lunch?"
Or, I can say, "I like your shirt."

⑤

- -

I can talk about TV shows, food, sports, shopping, pets, weather,
and field trips.
There are a lot of things I can talk about with my friends.

⑦

6 If we are on the bus in the afternoon, I can ask, "What are you going to do when you get home?"
Or, I can say, "I have a ball game tonight."

I will work on meeting
my goal - 10 ✔'s!

Make a ✔ each time you read your story.

My Favorite Thing to Talk About

by _____

Other people might not be interested in my favorite thing.
They have their own favorite things.

(2) My favorite thing to talk about is _____.
I could talk about it all day long.
I will draw it on this page.

When I talk to a friend, we take turns talking.
We talk about different things, not only my favorite thing.

This is how you have a conversation.
Sometimes I talk.
Sometimes I listen.

(5)

It is important to remember that I cannot talk about my favorite
thing all of the time.
My friends and I have fun when we talk about many things.

(7)

6 We will talk about many things.
This is what friends do.

I will work on meeting
my goal - 10 ✔'s!

Make a ✔ each time you read your story.

Giving Compliments

by _____

When I tell someone that he is a good artist, I am giving him a compliment.
I can say, "Great picture!"

③

2 When my friend tells me she likes my shirt, she is giving me a compliment.
A compliment is a nice thing to say.

4 If I see someone helping a friend, I can give her a compliment.
I can say, "Good job helping your friend."

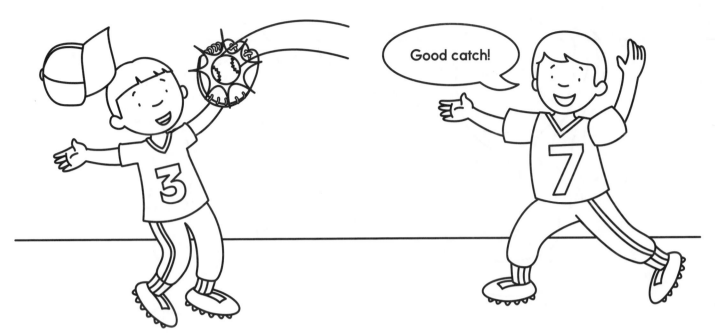

When I am playing outside with my friend, I can give
him a compliment.
I can say, "Way to go!"

(5)

People feel good when they get compliments.
I feel good about myself when I make other people feel good.

(7)

When I see that my friend's hair looks nice, I can give her a compliment.
I can say, "I like your hair!"

(6)

I will work on meeting my goal - 10 ✔'s!

Make a ✔ each time you read your story.

Interrupting

by _____

Sometimes, I think of something I must say right away.
So, I interrupt my friend when he is talking.
This is not a good thing to do.

(3)

2 It is not good to interrupt people when they are busy.
I will try not to interrupt people when they are talking
to other people.

My dad said . . .

4 When I interrupt, I am not showing good manners.
My friend wants me to be a good listener.

Sometimes, I interrupt my parents when they are talking.
I feel like I cannot wait.
But, I will wait until they are finished talking.

(5)

I will wait until my teachers are finished talking.
I can raise my hand quietly to let them know I have something
to say or ask.

(7)

I may want to tell my teachers something.
But, they are still talking to the class.
I should not interrupt.

6

I may want to talk to my friends when they are busy playing.
But, I will wait until they are not playing anymore.
Then, I will talk to them.

8

52

I will make good choices when I have something to say.
I will keep my voice, hands, and feet quiet if it is not my turn to talk.

(9)

GOOD JOB!

Everyone is proud of me when I don't interrupt.
I feel good about myself when I use good manners.

(11)

(10) I will try to wait quietly.
When the talking is finished, I can say, "Excuse me."
Then, I can talk without interrupting.

I will work on meeting
my goal - 10 ✔'s!

Make a ✔ each time you read your story.

54

Using My Words

by _____

Sometimes, I forget to use my words.
When I forget to use my words, no one knows what I want.
I feel upset when people do not know what I want.

(3)

(2) It is important for me to use my words.

- -

It is easier to get along with other people when I use my words.
When I use my words, other people know what I want.

(4)

I can use my words to talk to my friends about a game we could play.
Or, I can ask a friend if she would like to have lunch with me.

(5)

I can tell the doctor where it hurts.
Then, the doctor will be able to help me feel better.

(7)

6 I can ask my teachers for help.
I can tell them what I do not understand.
Then, they can explain my schoolwork.

8 I can tell my family what I did in school.
They are interested in what I do.
They will enjoy my story about my day at school.

I can tell my teachers when I need to use the restroom.
Then, there will be no accidents.

9

When I use my words, it makes my teachers, family, and
friends feel happy.
It makes me feel happy too.

11

I am glad I have a new brother.

(10) I can use my words to talk about how I feel.
I can tell if I feel angry, sad, or happy.
I can tell why I feel this way.

- -

I will work on meeting
my goal - 10 ✔'s!

Make a ✔ each time you read your story.

TIME TO BE PROUD!

Name

has done an AWESOME job communicating with others!

Date

Signed

TOP TALKER!

has risen to the TOP of the communication ladder!

Name

Signed

Date

_____

by_____

- -

_____

_____

_____

_____

_____

_____

- -

I will work on meeting
my goal - 10 ✔'s!

Make a ✔ each time you read your story.
